FEAST

Tomaž Šalamun

Feast

POEMS

Edited by Charles Simic

Foreword by Edward Hirsch

HARCOURT, INC.
New York   San Diego   London

Translated from the Slovenian by Joshua Beckman, Michael Biggins, Marko Jakše,
Phillis Levin, W. Martin, Christopher Merrill, Andrew Wachtel, and the author.

Library of Congress Cataloging-in-Publication Data
Šalamun, Tomaž.
Feast : poems / translated from the Slovenian by Joshua Beckman . . . [et al].
p.   cm.
ISBN 0-15-100560-5
I. Title.   II. Beckman, Joshua.
PG1919.29.A5F4   2000
891.8′415 21—dc21   99-043961

Designed by Lori McThomas Buley
Text set in Dante MT
Printed in the United States of America
First edition
A C E G I J H F D B

CONTENTS

Grateful acknowledgment is made to the following publications, in which some of these poems first appeared.

Alaska Quarterly Review: "Little Mushrooms"; *APR:* "Triumphal Arch," "Three Wise Men Cannibals," "Bingo," "Go," "Jure Detela"; *Black Warrior Review Chapbook:* "(what's your favorite color)," "Words," "Žare," "There's Raspberries," "March 22, 1993," "The Hill," "Seven," "War," "Trieste, Alexandria, Saint-Nazaire," "Sonnet of Power"; *Boston Review:* "Letter to Artaud"; *Conduit:* "The Castle," "Man-Sheep Stock"; *Grand Street:* "My Glass, My Flour," "Hvar," "(A flight of a bird)"; *Harvard Review:* "Carnac," "Mamma Merda"; *Heat* (Australia): "(What's your favorite color)," "Words," "Trieste, Alexandria, Saint-Nazaire," "Žare"; *The New Republic:* "Tell the People"; *Pequod:* "Now I would"; *Thumbscrew* (England): "Sonnet of Power"; *Trafika:* "First Day," "I," "Arrival in Saint-Nazaire," "Sweet Great Mother's White Hair Anthems," "They All," "For Jakov Brdar"; *Verse:* "Temple," "Jonah," "Fish-Peacock"; *The Whelks Walk Review:* "To give a scalp"; *Field:* "To the Princes of Darkness."

FOREWORD

Tomaž Šalamun writes a poetry of exuberant whimsy and
fierce rebellion. There is something deeply irreverent
about the work of this Slovenian poet who came of age
in the 1960s and now lives in New York City; something
freewheeling and stubbornly off-the-cuff—disruptive, en-
raged, uncanny—in his raids and flights, in his urgent asso-
ciations. He would refashion a recalcitrant historical world
to the heart's desire. "O God, for the day to come when
I / can mold the world with my Slovenianness," he calls
out at the end of one poem: "Able to play strong, dense
games." His poems constitute at once a series of playful
and ironic counterstrikes against history and a joyful mes-
sianic lyric.

Šalamun's poems embody his faith in reveries and
dreams ("A man must be judged by his dreams," he declares
in his self-portrait "I"), but one also feels in them the pres-
sure, the dark undertow, of human cruelty and suffering.
The headlines cry out ("Death glues a newspaper," he
observes wryly); Balkan wars hover in the background
("Human lives are fluff," he announces bitterly in "War":
"Lines of refugees, houses in flames"). There are down-
drafts of grief in these upward-sailing lyrics. Joy and suffer-
ing coexist in our world; they are simultaneous. As he puts
it in the introductory program poem "Words":

The sun strikes deep into the wells of the sky:
depends on how you look at it—for someone it is the hour
to be shot at dawn, for me the infinite gift

of red, of violet and bluish-graying white
above the bridge across the Loire.

Šalamun remembers here—he seems helpless to forget—
that someone is entering hell at the very moment he is
glimpsing paradise.

Robert Hass has pointed out that Šalamun's tradition
has been the disruptive, visionary side of European experi-
mental art. With Blake, Šalamun would say that "Energy
is eternal delight." He is an heir to Rimbaud (especially
the young seer of *Illuminations,* who asserted that "A Poet
makes himself a visionary through a long, boundless, and
systematized disorganization of all the senses") and Lautréa-
mont; to the Russian futurists and the German expression-
ists, to Khlebnikov and Apollinaire, to the French surrealists
who believed in what André Breton termed "mad love." I
also hear something of the improvisatory delight and daili-
ness of the New York Poets in these lyrics ("I breathe and
a poem jumps up," he says in a line that echoes Frank
O'Hara). Šalamun has blended and assimilated his Euro-
pean and American influences into a poetry all his own,
without losing his sense of gratitude and wonder:

I have a racket, air to breathe, clumsiness to protect
my soul and brilliance and Maruška and Ana and friends
to sleep with, my body and poetry.

Freedom is the first condition of Šalamun's poetry—the
freedom of the anarchic single voice, of the idiosyncratic
personal testimony. His poetry derails rational logic and

lyric elegance in order to delineate a stranger reality. He recurs often to the "infinite gift" of sunlight, to a blinding vision that is portal to other realms. "There is another world, and it is in this one," Paul Eluard asserted, and Šalamun repeatedly points to the existence—the intangible reality—of that other world. His "strong, dense games" are a way of gaining access to its mysteries. As he testifies in the concluding lines of this book:

> Along this window, in this window
> there are innumerable other civilizations,
> innumerable other cosmological systems.
> Thus suffering does not matter,
> layers do.
>
> This is what I show here.

I welcome you to Tomaž Šalamun's delightful and eclectic table. It is spread with impromptu secrets and timed surprises. It is overflowing with associations. Throw open a window, pull up a chair, and enjoy the imaginative feast.

—*Edward Hirsch*

FEAST

WORDS

Let them serve you champagne in bed,
the chilled one, as you awaken, still hot.
Rasputin smelled too much. Foscolo and

Leopardi, too—they built the steps for
Nietzsche—swim in the *Gai savoir*. Will tundra
suffer cyclically? Will the ice roar

when the little balls jet into the heart
of the Romanovs, like steam? The knight
combs his hair. He woke up lost in thought.

The sun strikes deep into the wells of the sky:
depends on how you look at it—for someone it is the hour
to be shot at dawn, for me the infinite gift

of red, of violet and bluish-graying white
above the bridge across the Loire. Yesterday
I had to write something for George Lambert Ristin,

he is very curious. The lights in town are not
extinguished yet, the duality flies above the sea gulls.
The sea gulls show their acne. They have long beaks,

they're trained for the mud beneath the marsh,
just as some canaries can dot and stipple. They're all
flying. Little frogs, snails, shells, Krombergs and

adoratus. A Malagasian reinstated the slivers of ships.
Small blacks climb on the shipwrecks, they saved
themselves from drudgery. The bourgeoisie

of Nantes ate slavery. They tramped over the ruins
with their wheelbarrows. Blessed little ribbons cut up
by little girls, the scissors returned to the baskets

lined with plush. Hangars are like skyscrapers.
The crunching of Scotch tape is related to the sun.
It creeps in silence. Strikes the window.

TRIESTE, ALEXANDRIA, SAINT-NAZAIRE

Gold coin in the cry of the sea gull rubbing against
the hair in my ear. Behind the chimneys, prose, behind
the bridge's girders, dawn. Kaisarion, in pink silk,
carrying hyacinths, was poetical. They all left
from here. Mayakovski, Nabokov, Desnos. Metka
and her mother stared at the *Normandie*, the cabins,
the common berths still arranged for war.
They embarked. There is no memory. Only
the one who sometimes looked like Toscanini, sometimes
like Chaplin, had memories. That's why Metka screamed at him
late in his life, like a cold-blooded murderer, why I
stood up and left, silently vowing to go into the night,
even at seventy, if I have to bear for one day
even a small percentage of that cold.

THEY ALL

"They all love me here, servants
included. I'll wire you Monday morning
after nine. I'll know by then. I'm afraid.
Your *s*'s are stressed too much. I'll take

this sweater, your wedding one.
I'll wait for the next bus.
Look, this is San Martin de Pores,
the small black man I was telling you about.

Is my scent nicer than that of your
kitten with white ribbon? I'm not an angel,
I'm a man who wants to experience
that experienced by the one who gave us

life. We are seven children.
My father is three years younger than you.
When I leave you'll get sleep, so your heart
won't betray you. So you won't lose your wife."

ŽARE

Artaud was throwing up, Artaud was killing
himself. I'd like to dance in the disco again.
Like when I saw the shiny copper floor.

I followed a group of people. Plundered the new
anchorage. I was waiting for Sonja, learning
Spanish. Renting a bicycle was cheap. I

walked anyway. Then Kali and Star arrived
and Bojan and Živa. She drew carpets. Does
God guide the fish? Who suffers from the memory

of twisting? The dead impose on the living.
The living, as long as they're alive, don't
die out. We were eating. We were rocking

the newborns to sleep. Near the low walls,
which were carefully built. The walls to the east
were less solid. People have darker eyes in Cyprus

than in Crete. More like olive trees. They rise
from the earth like burning snakes. The trees also burn.
Bushes, the basilica, stones, all remain black.

Then the rain fertilizes everything. In the country
people touch more. The mothers aren't shy, they wrap
their newborns' penises angling upwards. Thus

one can strike and thrust and, standing,
not give way. Women depend upon pleasure.
Me, I was staring at the bicycle. She didn't watch

Buñuel closely enough, she evaporated, she
couldn't control herself. Never again did I have
a bicycle like a Dunlop. On the slope of Belvedere-Isola

I extracted a stone like a tooth. The bicycle felt only
a scratch. We missed the steamboat. Olive trees
don't smell like eucalyptuses. The trembling of eucalyptuses

is too horrible. Horrible as dust. With their long leaves
they strike. Olive trees are stronger, cows lie under them.
When a cow arrives, the cab leaves. Even now Žare's swimming

on his back. He prefers to lie peacefully
on the water, collecting Andro. He says
he's hardworking. (È molto bravo.) He doesn't drink

anymore. His son is in electronics
in Trieste. It was Phaebo, when his little head fell on the oilcloth.
They had an enormous flat above the drugstore.

His father-in-law took it over. He proclaimed it his
property. My floor evaporates. I drop heavy balls.
I don't know how to juggle them properly.

Whoever eats from the Tree of Life loses all his sins.

MARCH 22, 1993

A spiral was distilled.
On the interior of the vault of an ant's foot,
city-cubes, crushing heads are growing.
Stabbed are those in the silver horizon of the plains.
Spit turns over the flower bed and for the flower bed, the guitar.
A cathedral kneels, crumbles like a bale of hay.
I install myself in the bones.

I breathe and a poem jumps up.
There are demolished stoves in the tub when the sky is
    stretched.

He starts with a typical intrusion into the resin
and black lava covers him.
In the mental vaults there is only a sexual
substance. There is no other.

If you bind wire around a chicken, surrounded by
light blue, blue, bright red and
yellow hoops, will there be more breathing there
than at the breaking of the insteps
of wellborn Chinese girls?

A spring day rinses out the smog.
A box has eyes.
A Cherokee has a fire hydrant.
What you drink in the gravel ...
The Lord sent me a caterpillar to stop me.
The Lord smuggled me into a caterpillar.

I'm watching myself, I've acquired the rhythm of giants.
It rustles, it makes a noise, the mass spreads out and licks.
Water cracks because the dam breaks.
Kalpas look for boat-building materials.
No, not Kalpas! We'll fly! Water is
soft as an egg.
Stove—leafy pastry.
Between rakes there is hair, ants.
Vinyl is piled up into pyramids.
This is a biology lesson, how animals are different.

No one said the cosmos is not a box that, through
pillars of salt, drinks the sun like nitrate.

And everyone reading this, beware! Don't fall into the little oven!
With the saliva! Become a flower bed in spring! And stop.
Not for the highest stake.
The castle has a terrible face.

THE CASTLE

It roars, it howls and whispers.
It pulls out so it hurts.
I do not hear, the light is thawing.
I see how pieces of me are eaten away, I swim.

I belt myself in, diving into
your sky, our Oneness.
You are the sheet, the father, the lava,
the azure prince of my dark crust.

I dress you in my wreath.
Bang you into the power plant.
While falling you burn in water,
landing in my palm.

Ear, ear, the deer's ear!
I eat out of Brandenburg.
Lift you from the continent
with my nostrils, breathing in

terrible food. Will I
promise you with my hand?
A fresh stain, a gift on an already
resewn head. One

hears my horn from
inside out. Crystal horses,
soft black bottles.
The whole castle is kneeling.

DOLMEN

O view from the window, at daybreak
from the tenth floor, of the sea,
of the lighthouse and freighters in Saint-Nazaire.
The same view: from Keller's bar, at the end of Christopher
Street, of freighters sliding on
the Hudson as here on the Loire.
Here Olympian and slow, there
juicy and fresh and black,
a black man who cried in my lap
brought me there.
The red mouths of black men are silkier than the mouths
of white men, softer, more terrifying, more
tender and deeper. More like the mouths of calves
from Karst, which die in innocence before
they're slaughtered.
You're my stone, Kosovel.
Resin, ropes, fences,
tar and the silent sliding of tires.
You hear it more than the breakers.

The coin, which silently circles, falling and rising
in the alcohol, it's not you hissing, it's the gasoline hissing.
Why in the flocks and why do they scream?
They tear themselves apart. Soda water shreds sight.
As long as the green doesn't calm down again,
o plush of beads.
You barely touch the stick with the chalk.
The sea behind the glass is the other pole of collision
and drinks it. People rip themselves apart.
Rip like scarves. This continent is
big. It can smash your lungs

if it catches them. Here the Atlantic is
massive and gray, fed by
the Loire. Stones furrowed like eternity and
old. The fresh beasts along the Hudson, one
next to another, tear the mountains apart, avidly,
the sea is still too young to calm you down.

ON A PAINTER'S CLOTHING

This is not a shirt, this is
an atlas. It was stripped off,
folded, twisted up.

It fluttered. A giant
perforated it. Every
morning, when she

put it on. Does it
subdue the beats of your
heart? And my old pants, which

you mend, patch on
patch, only your father's
from Bari had more

patches. Good that we
got on so well. That you can
combine shirt

and pants. When he
died he was like
God.

Like a rebellious
child, fresh in
death.

HVAR

Let it rattle in my arms, in processions,
like an eel rushing from the mouth of the sun.

FISH-PEACOCK

With juice in my muscles.
I'm not bad, I'm used to it and calm.
I'm dissolving my eyes.
I hear the sail fluttering.
The sun kisses the white linen
thirty times and settles
like a glowing club.
Who cares about *refoli!*
From the left and the right—the sea!
A quadruped first uses all
four legs, he runs over the earth.
The bush scratches, how it stomps, now here, now
there, but what steps into silk,
a rift in the glue, still on the earth?
Is it still in triumph and juice when it takes off?

No one scratches you softly in heaven. You
can't roll up your cloven foot,
no granite cube for your
head. Moldering limbs have meaning.
The air is grayish bronze,
someone is burning linen tablecloths,
the calves are drunk and dazed.

You catch your lungs,
they roll over and uncover
a fresh cherry pie, someone
unwinds it before it was poured
into the piepan. Plants grow
into it and out,
the skin fits like the moon.

Do you remember my blue bathing suit
and the record for the hundred-meter freestyle?
How you stretched above the splits.
And your rested pulse,
a little like a twitching fish,
a little like a fish fanning itself.

VIOLENCE AND LOVE

I come in chains. As a series of numbers, as
the weeping of flowers. A white body on a black landing,
I don't like brown with black. Can the gust of sound

from a car be scattered like feed for a hen?
Messages pave their roadways. Where did I
bind you up? Where blood doesn't flow to?

You are in two bodies, as in two bowls. I am
a mushroom. I erase the blackboard. Optical cables,
huge brown pyramids; film it when the signs

break through. The bloom collapses, dries up,
drops the way a crutch will slide. Who is taking sides
in molasses? How does food comfort hunger?

How does form—shutters, a wall collapsing because of
salt, a fugue of stone on the pavement—tell
your palm's sediment? Gondolas. They are on their backs.

The dove pecks them tenderly. And when you sigh,
as when the bellow stretches—you endured
the shape. Before death there is *zucker*. The kitschy

stones of Mary at Lourdes, mother of God, and the dazzling
asphalt surface in front of Fatima do not disturb.
The voice is clear. The voice is formed.

JURE DETELA

Do you hear grief through the language?
You throw dust as Hindus do.
Who is wounding an insect? Your
stomach, an overgrown ruin in
Chateaubriand in the German woods.
Or Hugo in a coach, registering everything
while violently fucking?
Not the Lake poets.
Leather is heavy. Do you
hear grief through the language?
I am still angry at you and your
long gazelle-like leaps.
You were an athlete,
destroyed by your zest, by
us who were too frightened
to touch you.
We were only breathing and smoking,
surrendering to the shower of your voice.
Brains—azure blossoms and wild dogs—
raised the wall of your body.
You bribed them. Out of
zest you squeezed me and
scared me into admiration.
While you were alive,
I didn't stand for my right to be carnal
and despotic, to be clear
in my hunger, and defeated.

FLEEING

I am shaking with the wrathful wound of Pards.
O lagoon! Where Alexander basked in the sun, naked.
Measure: the Himalaya's whiteness, brushes,
dancers' ankles. Did
Nureyev breathe in the pool?
Did membranes between hills and valleys
bind that early morning? Smooth surface.
The earth's crust had a maximum of two meters
above sea level, the soldiers didn't climb.

Tigers were cats.
Soldiers were not alone.
Then from where does the red stock come
that your soldiers pressed
into the abandoned valleys of India?
Who anointed Croesus?
Who defined peace above water
and millennia for amber to mature?
Do you think memory will lose its scent?
In that rare spot—hidden at Lake Bohinj—
where you both got suntanned. Before the marriage.

While escaping, to what did you return?
Are you so lost you cannot come back?
What was the angle between the sun, Pršivec
and the speed of your two bodies turning?
Did you almost bring him?
Did your twelve floors turn around,
each on its own axis, and
cut through breasts of a random wanderer
in the corridors?

Balustrades, unclean of blood,
and Turkish carnations in the screes.
Look son, my pulse is watching you,
you don't take your bone off unless
it gets rotten.

The snow goes under the sleeves and under the sweater.
The roasted apple reminds us of the Tatars.

WATERFALL

He talks like a gutted coin,
he dives headfirst into the jaws.
He doesn't move the moss on the tree trunk,
he only wipes the covers off the skin.
The eyes drink up the model,
they mate with other facts.
Or they lie for a century under the earth
like ore, unnoticed.

The moss gurgled in and gurgled out,
drawing contour lines.

There will be no more chairs.
They will only be in our mind,
and when you sit down
your body will receive no signal that
you're sitting. If you want you can imagine
you're a monad with your toes nailed together
spinning backwards on your axis.

The green leaves of the beech in spring—
one minute taken from the inner courtyard—
make footholds for toes
with rainbows in them.

MAMMA MERDA

Geniuses are abhorrent, terrible, monotonous,
they remind me of the jaws of a turtle.
Pieces of shit are for people.
Shit is kind when you push it out.
It stares, it doesn't worry.
It smokes like a pig.
It reminds me of the white heights of mountains made of
    amber.
Of Gregorčič, for example, actually
of myself and the bloody Soča river.
Only a divine frenzy can excuse this.
That's it, a divine frenzy is a democratic
institution, the property of all, mostly
of kids and four-year-old cousins.
They come to family reunions and say
shit, taken by a sublime joy.
They shiver and roll around in happiness and
divine rapture and you say ooops! that's not
fair, I'm the father, the parent,
I made flesh and can't play
with them and if I fall into the role of my
son I'll push him away and so I'm squeezed against the wall.
You're innocent as long you're untouchable,
better not to loiter
near those blotting papers
surrounding you—
shit is my brother, sin is terrible—
with the sons.

GOD

I
stole
a
piece
of
meat
from
a
live
friend
and
doled
it
out.
Whatever he is, I am too.

DINNER BEFORE DEPARTURE

The one! The divider of motion! Two is a horse's
neigh, a dusty cloud. Him, the soft one, in between
the mouth of the berry, and Him, the hard one,

son of the high tide. The one gives shapes to trees,
to groves, to sunlight in the hut, opens a parachute and
exhales it. Lightens heavy breathing and flavors it

from within, like lungs with marmalade, its paws
soft and supple, pink. You sledded over
his heart. You stamped on his wound with moon

boots. You filled up the living, the crying
of your own thigh when the staircase roared.
Newborns cried, wakened by the haze

when the fire shot to the second floor, above
the surface. Do you remember Rob
Favre, who described all the flights of my birds?

Clucking at Dobyns, pondering. The ribs
of the room were visible. Pieces of your
stairs slowly fell into your sack. And

the earth gave birth to harmonicas,
cakes, valleys of fertile mud, linked to what you
offered with your eyes still closed. Pontoons

were always the critical point (Plato calls stars
animals) of buttonholes and of a jacket. Celestial
bodies are always lapping, building a stake

on which to burn Bruno. Did you know
he breathed like a cable? His protector couldn't
stop him. His silken loot was drying along the channels

and the consulates. Do you think I'm already marching
beyond my lung capacity? Remember the snowstorm,
the car that was too wide, the night before Canada. Pine

needles at the gas station in Portugal. The arguments
here are only because of the air, only because
of the *opritchniki's* trumpets. In fact the road is straight

and spurts lotuses. A step and cascades. In great
rose hall sleeps the One, uncovered. The cotton wool
you wore out in the five years you were mute.

LETTER TO ARTAUD

Joseph! Joseph! He called him. He built froth
for himself in the bread. With a bibelot of salt, with two
bibelots of salt. He wrung out his breath.

Rocks were cutting. Jacob, if he's in a box, doesn't
jump. He picks. He picks and pokes, sows mortal
dew. The little ball rotates in the tonic. The sun

curdles before it gets white-hot. Two wells, one
below the other. There was glitter, with a membrane,
with little hills. They didn't spill over, they lay

in the belly of the earth like two fat drunken snakes.
They didn't touch Robert. Robert, Jacob,
Joseph, we all got our teeth into it. Muzzles kept

falling around thighs like foxes. They solidified
into ceramics. Ceramics are the eyes of cathedrals. Under
the foot of every elephant is an eye. The eye is harder

than the fan. The pheasant covers your
eyes. Its chest is a thick plank. Then I yanked terraces
out of the hills. I yanked out every grain of rice. The meat in

aspic and the stench open. Cotton rags absorb linen.
Then we pull them out with a cord. With a musical ear
from the well below, and from the one above with a bucket

and a cord. *Trictrac*. The skin rubs itself out. When the cube
spins on the flat unmarked field, it spins for the last time.
The oblong triangle draws itself. Then a round

token drops out. This one jams. This one jams.
At the same time soothes. I hope,
I really hope, someone stuffs the heads of the Indians

with vinyl plastic. Only then will they be able to stick out
their tongues, first at the backs of the ants, then at
the bone of the sun. The bone hangs like a monument.

GO

Go.
Grind up the pure light and wipe it away.
Step into the pure light.
It's there, it flutters like a flag.

It kneels.
No need to melt it down again.
It's everywhere, in the humidity.
In the white gill of the silver thread.

There is a saying: it lulls you.
You can make a little nose from the light.
Which breathes boats, graves and air,
the wall of the white we.

ARRIVAL IN SAINT-NAZAIRE

He thinks he'll recognize me, and he does.
The arch rises above the trains. The landscape is old.
The houses are low. We are both interested.

We start smoking immediately. Immediately
Langhe swims to the surface, the narrow door
of the fortieth anniversary, his daughter

et les Juifs. We drink, we start to address
each other with *tu.* I want to read him, to
devour him, to give him back his arteries.

To carry him off like a barbarian. To cut softness,
respect and sadness out of him. I want to explain
to him the ardor pouring over one beyond this

door. Power and light, *amour fou* of ripe age.
And the enemy, logic and elegance, the beaten track
of the perfect instrument. You have to crush it,

to walk through it. I'll give him all of this.
Breathe him, watch him, crush him to pieces.
Because I miss what I threw away. The weight

of the imprint. Even so I'm stronger than he is,
wilder, I can tell him more, I can lead him
better, and first I'll almost kill him on the rapids

to restore his courage. He needs some
Russians. Someone who still smells Mexico. But
for me, this is the ideal view of the sea.

The wound will be a fabulous pool. And it's also
far away. Ladinos, Marranos, Sephardim, we have
heavier and duller memory than the Ashkenazim.

O God, for the day to come when I
can mold the world with my Slovenianness.
Able to play strong, dense games.

MOSS

Evil. Spirit. Hair. Suspicion. A beam.
Points caught fire. With a plow I sink into white
flour. Amino acids are colored. But the breath?

There are ants in the mushroom. In the shearing of
washerwomen's flights, cubes on whiteness. Is
the cube on a sheet, honey in cut pear?

Little god's child in the violin's box.
Is this Moses' basket? Birds that peck you
out of a boat? Pink claws, they are Šuševi's.

The Nile got wet in Orinoco. I'm covering my
tracks. The snow started to flutter on the
stake. The twenty-seventh of January he hadn't

asked for grace yet. He didn't sign. Not for
a drop he didn't sniff my crust. Are you
deluding yourself that he will obtrude you

a roof? He'll be denied. The one rolled in
the silver in the dew in the picture.
Il est ému, mon amie. I started to smoke in your

honor. Well, but if we again pile up grass,
unfold covers, in what will the canvas be sky?
Branches get peeled. Do birds fly away shrieking?

Are not vestments, ash in August, eyelids (thirty
eyelids nearly cover the shore),
made like mammoths and little brooms? To make

a new hole in a belt is as to build a new castle.
To call mirrors. To panel doors. To wear out
horses while supplying wood. Can you

abdicate now like bubbles? Don't you
think you smell a bunch of flowers? Why
the brocade should not already be here? It glues.

So the sandal is stuck in the little stable. If
you want to proceed, you'll have to go barefoot.
The hammer got misty. I opened the window,

scattered little eggs. They were falling along
creepers when linen flew. How are notebooks
born? Who throws blue lines into them?

Do you think you can read the ways of ex-nests?
There must be a place where they come from.
They chase away and they are flat. They subside

exactly there. On that white paper. Are there
no traces of saliva? Does nothing take leave,
does nothing die? No traces of sea froth?

Like a woodcutter wiping the axe. He goes
toward a boat's womb, leans against it, searches
for a violin. He lies beneath the angles of

moving trains. The stars are catapulted into my
body. They rub off like little white balls.
I have yellow ears. I'm a father the way I hear.

Will you protest? Will you soak your hands
in the finger. Look, the scythe didn't cut
my belly. I eat dog-rose berry. I eat

turnips. If this were marimba it would
slip right there. But it's a cart, a colored
statue of a territorial guard. "I grope for

health in the cave." Is this
how the surface (dish) and a monumentality
of stalactites talk in darkness?

A million years only in that direction. Then
a smile, let's say two meters burst, and then
again a long recollection of a shift in silence.

Every one thousand seven hundred years crickets
bump into it. Their eyes get pierced by
silverware. You are sawing in the yellow color.

It's truly dangerous. I will bandage your fist.
You will walk like worn threads of devil's
hoof. Don't scream. There is no haptic sky.

CARNAC

In his hunger he uses many feathers. Myth
sews and sells him. A cruller twists
apart like a peephole. A beautiful girl
washes up. A robin binds a pale violet silk. Is
there a pebble in a peach? Is the pebble
the white Orpheus? Carnac has teeth and flames.
The morning makes a cross over the sea gull. The wind
speaks. It gives shape to what it rooted out.
The sun closes. White curtains framing
the dark night. The fire is closed and stored.
The murmuring slows. I see the grass
and the bare neck of a rooster. He watches over
the decanting of dolphins. The bone is inverted.
Tonight we sleep in paradise.

SACRED HEN. LA NOTTE DI
SAN LORENZO

The white meat is torn from the little bones, the dark is
heavier, it doesn't float. My arm will burn. When it drips,
it will smell of me. The belly is soft and hot.

When you gasp, I push my soul into you as if it were
a stamp glued on a tablecloth which I put into a transparent
plastic bag full of warm water. Finger in the water to unglue

the stamp. Under the parquet, the ground, under
the ground, the snack bar. Nothing there. The spurts
are your bright snickers. I should begin to write

that the cuirass is wet, loose, that you step away, that
you don't grab it, poof! like a fool, you barely touch it.
At the start of the night I'm blessed, in my dreams heads crack,

yellows and reds squirt up from behind the mountains,
then a zone completely black, dead, to wake me up
and make me ask what died. Then again, I'm boiling

in the pot and water simmers and I wait to see if we
really made it out. Language is a hook, it catches nothing.
I'm too young to be humble. They cleaned up my machine.

The body ate the flesh of language. Poof! I send a train,
a steam engine. It runs to widen you, finally you
split in two. Hooked to your body, it goes no further.

The steam engine leaps. Only it should come out
at the neck. I would like to keep the head clean, the skull
with all the skin, all the hair, all your arranging of your hair.

I felt blood under your chopping block. The doe turns

into a bird and takes flight. It's heavy. It barely
gets off the ground. Branches rub the belly of the doe,

which is now gray. I'd like such a bar. No need to be a grill.
It could be a grill through which water drains from the street.
A little bigger. I'd put you there. I'd set a fire underneath.

JONAH

Pleasure writes history. Bombs resemble
human eggs. You tear them off and throw them
around. They rut. Shepherds wake in the hills.
You see, a grenade falls on your head, it's landing there.
The ones who were served grew bored. Still I never
saw a whale. Supposedly it swims in the sea. Supposedly
you can stick a mast through its eyes. Yesterday
they killed my darling Jeffrey Dahmer
while he was cleaning a toilet. He had eaten
seventeen young men and ended in blood. Power
is always inherited, never divided. And if a body is unraveled
we mend it. Power cannot evaporate. It renews itself
on solemn scaffolds. We, the people who wade in blood,
we're erotic and fascinating. We write sublime poetry.

TEMPLE

1

Where there is nothing to say
the light of disappearance exists.

2

Time moves.
Lava glows.
I am underneath the gutter, a silent mushroom.

Copper rocks.
The flame is mute.
That's for me.
Terrible.
That's for me.

3

Little corner, little red dry corner.
Who is the spring?
I'm buried here with you.
Thus I have everything.

4

Like Buddha I gaze into the motionless.
Into the mosque and rock.
I'm taking hands.
I drink the Sava River.
I see a cocked hat. I draw straws.
My head is very small and hairy.
You speak to me. You speak to me.
I'm tied up with the wedding guests.

5

Happiness makes me vomit.
Who are these quiet white horses?
God, how round you are.
How kind.

6

The position of the thorn in your crown,
the mill stopped in the rock.
In the apple, in the seed,
no mouth for you under the sky.

7

Time doesn't investigate
those frozen by the hours.
No cascades for the gentle ones.
The savage doesn't lie on the shield.
And the thunder that poured out of your mouth
fattens gems.
Crumbles the door of hesitation.

8

The foam on the muzzle speaks of pain.
I dry the cow.
Pumpkin, do you hear me?
I have no one else.

9

Your fire, brother to your
brother, was disfigured in the sun.

WAR

First, ice. Then pine woods.
Then ice again. Human lives are fluff.
Lines of refugees, houses in flames,

shrieks like the scratching of colors on the skin
of salamanders for a billion years. I want
a yellow spot. Now the sun is sprained.

We think a lot about where our paws are.
Rungs on which wheat stalks strain? Red
powder is enough. A little sulphate is enough.

And the smoothness of china—will it hold? Dregs
of coffee, as if poured from the buckets of giants.
Odessa is built here. Here are hunting dogs.

A crown in the breast of time. The secularized
version: how the chicken rotates on the spit.
A windowpane yields no warmth. Who

made it transparent? Who owns the energy
nibbling under the teeth? Have you ever spilled
a bucket in the desert? Like throwing snow to the hens.

THE HILL

The hill is insufficiently tested shadow
because the snake bit the news vendor. What happened?
I went to sell a few copies and of course I had

to shout. Sometimes I limp, but only when there are older
women. I belong to Primož's generation; I was his
schoolmate; torpidity gives me pleasure.

I take the elevator then pace the corridor.
I meet white people. Death glues a newspaper.
Are you cuddling with someone? Did you

sleep well? Did you go to the movies?
Did you throw your towel away? *Mihi*
tibi a volute. More tribes go into the sand.

You can't have both shutters and venetian blinds.
You can have them on different windows.
But then you should also have the seas

and the North and South, which can
rotate in the white angles, in the white
saddles. Everything is unraveling. Everything

follows. In God is gush and juice again. Ardor
is in mustiness. The juxtapositions of miracles
resemble starched threads hanging from the white

sky. Bristles when the cosmos sweats? A fat
pig that doesn't open its skin until we're dying?
Some whine in their folds of skin. Some

know everything and would like to start smoking.
Some talk softly, they see and slide back
and forth. They don't say much but it feels like light

snow. It's beautiful. Your delicious bone loses
its mind. Does it suit you not to have any plans
with me? You wouldn't even notice. I would.

My white darling, my little well-behaved, watch
how I walk uphill. Maybe you come like a torch,
with a white wall, with two flames. Maybe

the sea gulls shat on your cap. You're a pumpkin,
the snow in the apple, the tiny bell that rang
in error when you came to take the neighbor away,

NKVD. Do you want me to warn him
with a broom? Do you want me to lay him
on the sidewalk with my hands? Fluff in my teeth.

Give me both shirts. The one that cracks and
smolders and the one that melts in the mouth. Let
me crawl on all fours then bounce, not totter.

Let me, from all fours, take off at a sprint and just
before the wall land on my back. Not falling.
Not turning around but doing a half-flip.

FIRST DAY

1

You will see rivers on butter in Vilnius.
We will call you the quenched.

2

Files are for soot.
In the light lying on the cheek.

3

If we had eaten a slipper, we would draw it on the
    blackboard two times.

4

Send off for a baking tin.
A baking tin should pick up a baking tin by itself.
One kilo of bread and one kilo of fish: two of them.

5

Washed flesh is an expense.
Little balls are dancing.

6

A soul on wood feels like a newsboy.
It's anchored in the clouds.

7

Ditto is like someone squeezing a hooter.
As if bees would run away.

8

A wrinkled poppy is on fire.
A heavy beam is flying from oil to lead.

9

You didn't twist your groin with a pacifier.
Little sleeves started to float.

10

An iota smells of grazes, of lemons, of
snowballs, of a metronome.
Dwarves and giants slap their faces.

11

Dry out the righteous.
He'll rub out all of your hair.

12

The heart travels in sand with a wire.
Buddha mildly lactiferous.
With whitened hills.

13

If I drew tusks to an owl others would erase them.
Tolerance is the cherry in a cherry stone.

14

Do small frogs flash when they jump over,
and what do they jump over?

The flight of a butterfly in the open.
Snow is fragrant.

15

A shepherd stepped down from the printer
and established an icy lake for himself.
There are shoelaces and small ribbons on the crust
as *bora* seduced them.

16

A stung town overflowing its shore
sails around the world.
From the heart to the heel.
The vault collapses.

17

Effectuate *courant d'air.*
The dead are to be thrown on rags.
Only wet lakes survive in the horizontal.

18

How to weld time?

DUMA 1964

Fucked by the Absolute
fed up with virgins and other dying sufferers
I love you o neighbors, meek fantasies of God the Father
I love you o integral characters of sweet gazing
in my mind grace yielded

o proud possessors of anxieties
o trained intellectuals with sweaty little hands
o logicians, vegetarians with the thickest glasses
o muzzled rectors
o ideologues with your whoring ideologies
o doctors munching on punctuation marks and Škofja Loka
    pastries
o mummified academicians patting passion and pain
Pascal who tried and Bach who pulled it off
o lusty inexpressible dried-up lyricist
o horticulture, the enlightened and the happy swallows
o socialism à la Louis XIV or how to shelter the poor little
    creatures
o one hundred thirty-five constitutional bodies or
    how to keep a dead cat from stinking
o the revolutionary zeal of the masses or
    where is the sanatorium to cure our impotence

I walked our land and got an ulcer
land of Cimpermans and pimply groupies
land of serfs myths and pedagogy

o flinty Slovenians, object of history crippled by a cold

LITTLE MUSHROOMS

So this is how the whole thing goes
by far the best are the little mushrooms
little mushrooms in the soup
nada nada nada nada

                        fiuuuuu one little mushroom
this little green parsley in tuxedo
and darkness for a long time
then they run to get a cleaning lady
responsible for all of this
nothing nothing nothing nothing

                        fiuuuuuuu one more little mushroom
healthy though
the blood is not so great
because she got hepatitis
Heavy heavy are these little mushrooms
heavy in the Holy Mother

WHAT IS NAUSEA

Nausea is when you come home
and say light the stove
and no one lights the stove for you
and it's February

oh come on oh come on
the worst nausea
is peas

THERE'S RASPBERRIES

We arrive at Karlovac
and start to talk about how to play
man to man
or with two centers
or the cross

and Guato has new sneakers
and the lights go on
and we all have our numbers
and Škinko is a fantastic guard
and they call time out
but nobody cracks our defense
and all our shots go down

but in the second half Aunt Agata
comes and says
oh
    oh oh how happy I am
and Olivieri comes
and says
oh
    oh oh how happy I am
and Auntie Lela comes
and says
oh
    oh oh how happy I am
Derin
Camerlengo
siora Pesaro
and they all walk up and down the bleachers
singing

oh
oh oh how happy we are

and you
are you happy with yourself
they ask me
as I throw the inbounds pass
and I think

sure
I'm happy
sure that I'm happy
oh
oh oh how happy I am

later the journalists ask me
so why did you lose the game

there's raspberries
raspberries

BINGO

Who are you who threw me into this country
who fixes my elevator
who feeds my hen and wears green earrings
who are you dirty little child
falling out of the window
collecting stamps or tearing down walls
who rebukes me for profiteering
fells trees eats bread with butter
who are you whom I see as a chimney
on the highest balcony from Palazzo Tacco
without frescoes on the bones
who are you imitating a tree
like a fig leaf
with a broken arm
the world silenced by roofs folded up wrong
who are you who arrives in a 1927 Packard
to uncover and cover your flesh
or walk in your stockings
bingo protected flower
child of the desert
who are you who in foreign pans
looks at your blood and flees down the fire escape
who buys land above the lake in Geneva
like Mr. Tavernier
and peels potatoes and
polishes buttons by himself
who are you who would die for the correct spelling
and in death would see how polenta steams
and on a plate how it steams
who paints the garden fence for the nineteenth time

but doesn't break up the spot in the night
an event in paradise Guy Patin
lost Buxton patent for keys

What's your favorite color?
my favorite color is yellow
would you wear a wig
if your hair fell out overnight
if my hair fell out overnight
I'd wear a wig
we heard you went to Portugal
could you give us some brief impressions
Portugal is a small country
the people dress well
was it hot
in the sun it was hot
even in the shade it was hot
did you have an uncle in the air force
I had an uncle in the air force
did he have an influence on your taking this job
I couldn't say he had an influence
he soon died and then he had no influence

Therefore they say if they are one and a half
times as strong as columns in a church
then these pillars are solid enough and
real if they were bigger the abovementioned
church would be darker and as for those
things that some quote out of ignorance
i. e. pointed arches are stronger and
lighter than the semicircular ones
and what was said after that about
other things the abovementioned master
asserts that art is worthless and worthless
are the arches be they pointed or semicircular
the center of gravity is in the towers they are
built upright because what is upright cannot
fall

I SMELL HORSES IN POLAND

I smell horses in Poland, ruins in Elbląg,
I smell water, blood, gigantic boards on shelves,
Juergen disappeared in the Tatras; by the time they found him
    with torches and bloodhounds he wasn't breathing
the frescoes in Campo Santo, every day I unload eight tons
I smell Manhattan streets, steam squirts, while banging my
    head on the roof of taxis
I smell gas, I smell icy mountains through the glass of a
    Lufthansa airliner
I smell Serbian epics, in Dečani, in Ravenna
I smell the earth beneath Hilendar, I sleep in Ioannina
I smell camouflage, I smell Monterey
the loathsome overcoats from the fifties, I play piano
I smell baseball in Brooklyn, the sperm of Cherokees
I smell logs for the Kočani-Čardaklija line, I wait and freeze
I smell the role of masseur, glass, physicists, garbage
I smell my stomach contracting in Nabrežina
I smell everything, arms, I smell lime, I pupate into Sanskrit,
    I smell Sufis,
the terror of local cultures, I smell angels
the white skin of family friends, I smell verbs
vanitas, I lay my tongue on a wheelbarrow, the smoke
    of Mancini
where old Bilbo touches the bank
I smell *concordance des temps,* smuggle Afghanistan
the races between Cassirer and Fatima, I smell whores on
    soldier's shoulders
gute nacht liebe Baberle, I smell Pika's corpse
I smell dressing up, a fossil, I smell sunrise
a Penguin selection, ants give off their odor

I smell cathedrals, proletarians,
Femme of Mrs. Mann-Borghese, I smell flattery
artifice and evil
I smell transgression, I sleep and I smell.

BOSPORUS

soldiery, a beam across,
Drava, Bosporus, fresh early drops,
glitter of water, decanting mimosas,
the man with the firm stance, deaf abbot,
white flesh of the redheaded girls, one meter of depth,
passage across two ramified thighs,
linen on a rope, sirens in the angles,
the earth doesn't move, mountains do not rest,
picture on the bus, turpentine on a threshold,
dry crumbling soil among precious stones,
a cross nailed into the pine, inland traveling,
pillar of smoke, lion between two young pages,
hell is oversalted, air among the vaults,
telepathy, with whose energy was the stone lifted,
drops with cotton, sea of sketched grass,
mighty vertical lines among the hay's directions,
bards, breaking of inflammable songs,
of safe mechanics, of tubes and helmets with a figure five,
o mighty flight of people colored in,
boys with cyrillic script, steps in reserve,
from Dutovlje to Tomaj is a hollow aperture,
a great cluster of low benches, glass of restless people,
tuxedo and England, Mostar and Cassiopeia,
salty nostrils of lineage, the smoke is rising,
an arrow, *pezzi di carne fresca,*
empty cans, slopes of blueberries,
I saw the deer when I walked uphill,
empty oil field, hair of flowers.

SWEET GREAT MOTHER'S
WHITE HAIR ANTHEMS

You had a cotton mouth since your birth, a tiny, tiny one.
O lilies that nibbled my hands, pierced my skin
and stripped, changed my veins into the body of another.

Me too, in this world, I rowed up the river,
crept on the bank in canto twenty-nine, worked out,
swallowed light. It didn't hurt. Everything was

blessed. I allowed the cracking of nuts, waited in honey
till the heart overgrew them. Changed rails. Let old yellow
trams go where they haven't been, crunching air a long time.

Human and animal flesh in the dissection room still lets out
screams: love me! still hear bales of wheat, trucks, cranes,
oils, containers' grinding and splashing in the harbor.

The bronze floor was boiling. O birds, bringing whales.
Dropping them on the guests' dark disheveled hair so the apple
burst, the plum burst, the grape burst. The juices mingled,

we became lotuses and little boats leafing through
towns on the water's surface. We smelled dust, saw
timbers, in the air, in huge fires carrying silt, lime

odor of burned and redeemed flesh, the blaze that made
the same decision as the gentle titmouse or the white skunk
and bolted away. Swam off, swam off as fish with wings,

as the jagged mouth. When you breathe in, does the earth
remember? Does it like shifts? Does your jell crack as sweet
molasses? Bruno, still my home and fire. My juice. My sweet
    womb.

FOR JAKOV BRDAR

The stone of a fruit opens, the child turns yellow and
falls. Boyars again and again cut our peat from
the earth. Whoever now leans over his shoulder
does not sleep. In fact, dredgers could not wound

nests and birds. We are the news. We drown in light.
We don't define the mirror, nor soft crusts in mouths.
The seal fell even before the bosom splashed.
Your knee, sculptor, stands. You repeat

the gesture of magma with your hand. You have
seed in your fingers and in your chest. You formed
the rib as fire, as people's laughter was formed.

We sit at the table, close to the barn, with the glass
of wine. On the floor faces rest, beings
bumped into your pollen gaze, and they are well.

I

I, after whom Ljubljana can be called antediluvian
and post-Šalamun, am full of joy, Arabic, so
please forgive me these lines immediately.
Homeland, women, bread of all kinds and tongues,
state prizes and agaves will come on the scene,
nonna, nonna's hats
and how I really think Mr. Bucik is a greater painter
than Jakopič, because he painted my mama.
What Mrs. Hribar said about my former boss,
how he nationalized the factory:
he was polite, absolutely charming, fucking and communism
beamed from his eyes at the same time, and Izidor Cankar
loved him.
I've no complaints.
And some incredible details from my underground life,
you'd be stunned, wow!
By thirty I got used to loving
everything. I have no dumplings in my throat.
I have a racket, air to breathe, clumsiness to protect
my soul and brilliance and Maruška and Ana and friends
to sleep with, my body and poetry.
And terrible pains, too, I kick them like a milk bucket.
Kardelj, I forgive him everything for hoping
Ljubljana would have millions of inhabitants
from people rushing into socialism.
A man must be judged by his dreams.
Toads, honey, the moon, willow trees, Split, the Baltic, *détériorer*
and I will never forget how we traveled from Krakow to
Gdansk.
The chief hires the hustler, bribes the train conductor
so the family sleeps soundly in first class,

wakes up with the sun in the north,
with sand, with Hanseats, with hawks and eagles,
and makes an arch to the Alps.
Where did we swim, chatting with effendis, Yiddishe mamas,
wrapped in shawls and eating cookies, with the mayor
of Mostar, where did we sing?
Madam's Nardelli garden has to be mentioned absolutely,
as well as her old Buick,
and how I'm wounded because of a talk with Hewitt,
John Deere's chairman who ate breakfast with Tito
and offered him a usurious rate of interest for tractors.
He says he respects Jagoda Bujić absolutely,
and that in the 1880s, when it all started, they were
clean-shaven until thirty and then hairy.
And,
il mio carissimo amico, di cui non posso pronunciare
il nome, il Dzoran, viene da lui?
Sure, but not for a fuck, lady, not for a fuck,
what is this St. Bernard doing, peeing?
Pino Pascali, that radiant beast, ocean liners,
Second Avenue, a myth, Third Avenue, light,
where are you, my dashiki?
Also put in the thing about San Domenico in Taormina,
and how I was smeared because of talking about it
with Roy McGregor Hasti, the fascist.
How we threw bombs in Rome
with Tomaž Brejc, and fled from the police.
How we still managed to shout to each other: if they catch us,
let's demand the Embassy, and if it goes all right, meet at nine
in the evening at Ivo in Trastevere.
And he said, you're an awful Italian, and it was
at five-thirty in the morning at Stazione Termini
when he arrived loaded with books that I would copy from

for Jonas, for the sacred aims of the revolution,
and I threatened to kill him.
From that time on, I've been flying planes and looking at the
    earth.
From that time on, I have a social security number
and am a renegade.
The greatest Slavic poet. Right.

MY GLASS, MY FLOUR

I drain this white body, froth for your glory,
crushed, I am volcanic, lord of your bronze wings,
slyly I eat you, when you are cruelest,
deep in the crime of forgetting me.

I caress you when I break your bones, when I spread you
over the granite like gray dust. I want to be free
and hungry again. I ground up your blood so fine
that it gives off no odor even in the deepest

membrane of my memory. Flower that shined
and left. No trace remains of us breathing together.
The terrible moistness of your veins is empty. There, where

I bite you. You died like the white silk of the blossom
on the pink magnolia. I pierced your arm, so that
our farewell flew away. I am your fragrance. Your neck.

THE EAST

Partisans of genre, the hoops around
the grain of sand were always made of steel.
Angels, a waterfall, and ruins serve
the bigger, stronger hordes that killed,

celebrating now the deaths of the enemy.
Shall I strip off Rome, a bulk that with a
transfer of weight into atoms implored
beyond its circumference, and then dispersed

itself in hateful autonomies, the decadent
burned out field, myth–hungry? I had
to cross the ocean by myself and

ultimately step into: who dies in
May is black as a silky elder tree.
The stars will splash like anthems.

There are five lights. A unicorn pushes his foot with a shovel.

RASPUTIN

Rasputin, shot, said:
o midges, iron dots,
sweet manna dripping from the hand of the Lord,
come in!
Neva said, get out, cow!

MAN-SHEEP STOCK

The upright, well-groomed ladies are responsible
for mythology. The visit of Maria Strozzi-Papadopoulos
in May 1947 to my grandmother in Voloska
made me into a foothold. Among all those
folding fans not destroyed by war,
among all those revolutions not butchered by
nostalgia, gazing at the bamboo wood,
I started to quake like a knight.
Mother, so terrifyingly pretty, sheltered,
still sure she doesn't need to inherit anything,
at that hour, not attentive enough to the flow,
lost the game at the terrace and
cut the wound. Because of her youthful ardor,
she thought I was to be the world architect
as a communist. With an open, clear soul,
we started to invite people's energy
to spend a night in our park.
But in 1947 the hatred of hats was already
a cliché. There were already those degrading
lists, father's turns of duty in Bulgaria,
despotical *tutoiements* which for
all my childhood made me
a wunderkind in piano playing, called *hochstapler*.
Even a long time later, this uncertainty
pushed me to fly jets around the globe,
to lament Europe and overdo my genius
in fear of being disinherited.
Because my mother's sin struck the general's wife
like a tiger, when the charm
was no more a question of the tribe,
but a question of losing blood.

You're a cry,
an exploded
heaven,

brother.
Your mind is torn by
gold and

wine.
You're rolled over by
monsters,

you eat
monsters. Lie down,
calm down.

Be shoulder to
shoulder with
the light, on guard,

you,
window-lamb,
lord of color.

Now I would
define myself
as Poussin.

He painted
something
awfully solid.

A good
painting
is recognizable

by not including
humor and
death.

Robert
Creeley and Tugo
Šušnik now

calmly
stare
at me.

As if
they,
before all

the others,
carried me on their
shoulders

and put me
down here. This
wall is for

this painting.
If I
sit at the

typewriter,
it is mother and guardian
angel,

if I sit
on the couch,
there is peace.

NOISE OF RAIN

A billion bums, nobody
sees beyond. In jail, I read
Ovid. I tried to be attentive
to militiamen. God, give people

spouses whom they won't beat and
children who will respect them.
It's almost Sunday. Ana is a long time
sleeping. I listen to the noise of rain

and, strictly speaking, living if you cannot
write isn't difficult. Yesterday was
a midsummer day. A friend's child
died before being born.

Then I went to sleep, the city was
bright to me. Below the window I
heard the voices of Paš's brothers
going somewhere with their friends.

SEVEN

Don't shove. The one who is cute enough,
a young deity, sooner or later
will enter my zone of interest.
Though there's not much to go on, the dead
do not speak, many things can be
grasped from my poems. This is my
principle: when the last Ibn Kabdul dies
I become Ibn Kabdul. When in
Alexandria there is nothing except
dirt and flies I become Alexandria.
Simpletons flap with the fact
that one day the sun will cool
and what will you do with your
manuscripts when there is no sun,
they ask slyly. Explaining to a knucklehead
the principle of immortality is the same
as asking a shoemaker to hew a table.
I don't do that. As I walk the town
I notice every prey about to ripen.
Cherries will redden.
Summer will come.

SONNET OF POWER

Let lips and flesh remember the arrival
of the bright, refreshed empire. Let it be
impressed on the eyes and in memory: playing with
wine and the flight of bees is for Pilate, not for
pathetic artisans. Let this massaging of people's
hearts and dripping of stalactites on their broad,
uncultivated bowels leave its seal on the green grass:
erasure. Therefore I ordered this delightfully
enticing nutriment to be inscribed. Let them
too become pupils for a while, that this impatient
stamping of the ground calms down and
surrenders to the natural order of things.
Events animated me completely. Let the placard
with my office hours be hung out publicly.

TO GIVE A SCALP

I mistake you for God.
Therefore I am a striated fluid in a big tube,
water inside your veins.
Like a walker, waiting for a metro in Atlanta
built by the French.
Open, dark, greasy rocks. The slate
itself. Where would you put it if it
poured over you? Would it flow off?
I see you watered by a red puddle,
with crust on your face, only your black
eyes are clean, nothing sticks to them.
There is oil on them, as they say: go backwards,
wash immediately. Then a layer of
gesso, you are lifting weights, I am
slowly lifting your little hands.
You remain hanging on them.
Brooks find their steady paths.
Deer stand in three to four centimeters
of water on the white stones,
drinking. The air is here. Everything
is dispersed. Now the crosses have Burgundy
heads, sealed veins. I skate with my chest,
turn it around. Little hen pigeons are still,
you keep them safe by breathing.

GAZA

When I'm thirty-seven, I won't go
bald. I
won't dress in white gowns with red
guts in my pocket.
When I'm thirty-seven, my mother
won't die. I won't
knock on the doors to my sons' rooms
with idiotic questions on my idiotically happy
face.
When I'm thirty-seven, I
won't work out at five-thirty in the morning,
snuffling like a
maniac. I
won't towel myself off in the village inns,
offending the pious ones who
barely survived the war. I
won't dress in knickerbockers. I won't
point to the Haloze and the lands they took
from us and say it is right.
When I'm thirty-seven, I
won't be on duty but
I'll be free. I'll grow a long beard and long
nails, my
white boats will sail on every
sea.
And if a woman bears me
children, I'll throw them through a
windowpane from the left corner of the
dining room and wonder
which will fall first to the ground,
the glass or the gauze.

THE TRAP

Gold doesn't evaporate,
gold isn't water.
Gold is eternal manure, because capital is
death which doesn't disappear.
I don't change,
only my value rises and falls.
In vain I wait for a man to crush
my mask, I'm only chasing
rabbits in the process called
the courtesy of wizards.
Dwarfs step up from my shoulders
in the process called
history, and there are only two things no one really
knows:
I'm everybody's lover, and:
where is the crime.

AN OLD SONG

If only
I may have,
at death,
a friend's hand
laid upon
my forehead.

TRIUMPHAL ARCH

Yesterday afternoon Giorgio dropped in
again. I took him to lunch.
He showed me the poems he'd written in the
morning. Then he called up Alfonso
at San Luis Potosi, 113A. Alfonso said
he'd wait for us on Calle Jalapa but we
missed each other. We made it to
his old colonial house and waited out
front. He arrived in a Volkswagen, his head
shaven. I knew immediately he was a magician.
He seemed to take an interest in me.
He took us through the rooms, we talked
about Lévy, Sir Randolph. He was telling me
about his Zen teacher, he showed me
the book he was finishing: *World Nutritional
Plan*. Then we smoked something
he called plain grass from Palenque.
I was holding his things—swords,
spheres, rope crosses, playing
with little bottles of mercury. He said he would
perform a little show for the two of us.
He danced, he played and blew,
grinning constantly. You'll be amazed
at the horrible power that kills, he said.
You won't be able to resist joy.
Now I'll continue writing my book,
he said, and drive you both downtown.
We got out at the Niza-Hamburg
crossroads. We started walking. I was astonished
to take such large steps, to breathe so deeply,
move so smoothly. Where are we going,

I asked Giorgio. We're going, he replied. Are you
scared? I said. He said he was sure
I wouldn't kill him. I didn't know anymore.
I felt the power would lead us
through the temple, that I would
eat his heart. We went somewhere to sit,
to have a drink, our mouths
were very dry. We went on foot,
upon a carpet. We arrived at Avenida Juarez,
Giorgio pointed at the immense Triumphal Arch
on Plaza de la Republica. There's my
hotel, he said. We walked for a mile
on a red carpet, a huge flag
fluttered from the Triumphal Arch. It was
November 20th, Día de Mexico. Where are we going,
I asked him. To the beginning, he replied.
They'll all be there, even the President of the Republic
and the Spanish King. I only felt my strength
growing, how I would first make love
to him and then eat up his heart. You know,
he said, Alfonso told me how
a snake once crawled before him. He stepped
aside yet the snake slithered toward him. It didn't
kill him, because he gave it all the power. Do you think
I am the snake now, I said. No, he
said, you're not a snake.
You're walking parallel to me. He pointed
to the right, away from the carpet, which led
to the eternal flame under the Triumphal Arch.
I grew sad. We walked for another hour
or two, the temple was always
on either our left or right. I remember
the sound of the fluttering flag. Then he

pointed to a window, that's my window.
You decide, he said. The Hotel Pennsylvania
is all in tile, all covered with blue
glazed tile. An old woman was
sleeping at the reception desk. Up in the room,
he smoked and said, it's your decision, it's up to
you whether to kill me or not.
I stopped undoing my belt. I stopped
taking off his boots. I lay down and
fell asleep. When I woke up, Giorgio was
sitting on the raffia chair by the wall,
crying. You're not the only one
who'd like to love, he said. I knew it was
done. I had drunk up his heart. I'll be
off now, I said. Giorgio's face was
radiant and beautiful. You see, he said,
reconciled. Light is for everyone. This
morning when I went out to breakfast, I
bought a paper, *Uno mas uno,* and
read that 383 Americans had committed
ritual suicide in the rain forest of Guayana
under the guidance of Jim Jones.

THREE WISE MEN CANNIBALS

I'm in a bar at eight in the morning,
200 meters from the house, looking at photographs
of the massacre of the People of the Temple, and I can't
decide. Then I just stop thinking and ring
the bell. The maid lets me in. Alfonso is still
in his nightshirt. His little sister giggles.
Their mother—Lebanese—took
the decapitated head of the old maid's father
to the police, wrapped in a shirt, and
the machete as evidence in 1952. Obviously
Giorgio is still sleeping, he isn't there. Alfonso says
first to Toluca, then to the hills. At nine
Giorgio staggers in. First we drank
pulque high in the mountains. A sour white
liquid from a barefoot Indian woman. I was looking
at the pines, which were just like the ones in Switzerland,
and the pointed yellow flowers, which seemed to drink
blood. In Temascaltepec we were leaning
against the walls of the houses. Alfonso was
talking about how he used to pan for gold around
there. We get in a car with Don Mauro who
takes his leave. Here he is, invisible smoke,
breath that will dissolve in the air. He
likes witnesses to his departures. His grandson,
waiting by his side, was also delighted
to see us. I drank pulque again,
noticing how the flesh of those people was open and
soft. Doña Lucia brings the chairs,
Alfonso talks about soya. The village teacher has
no idea how high these hills are. Then
we traded high fives, twice, high

and low. The sun burns. At lunch Giorgio
thought he could repair the jukebox.
The whiter people are in charge,
the Indians install the water line.
I'm eating. Under the table an eight-year-old
polishes my boots. The women wear their hair almost down
to the ground. What I remembered most were the white
teeth of all those people, and that we left them
a good tip. The ground is
covered with cobblestones. Alfonso knows many
of those waving to us along the path, hidden
up to their waists in the irrigation ditch. I see
the roots of the trees I saw somewhere
before. Some people mount donkeys
by the river where they wade. We ask where
the waterfall is. The sun is about to set. It's already
in the shade when we find the waterfall. Under it
is a circle, I must push off hard
to be thrown back to the surface again.
Giorgio already knows that, with one hand he grabs me
by the hair and says, this blockhead
is drinking. If I drink
fresh water when I drown,
I cough more than if I drink salt water.
Both Alfonso and Giorgio throw a stone
farther than me. They also dress
faster, even with wet skin.
I'm waiting for my skin to dry. I look
at the ground. I see the hoofprints of cattle
in the gravel, the sand, the mud. Beyond the noise
of the waterfall I hear the metallic sound
of the universe. It's also in the corn.
The same song. Alfonso is cold. We are climbing

back to the road. The sun is about to set.
There is red down in front of us, lots
of red. Ridges, crickets, steam.
I saw it in a dream. When I saw
a rider on a white horse, with a white
face, white hair, with
SAVIOR written in gold letters in
the air. Giorgio had already seen it.
I'm leaning against the Volkswagen.
We are not going to the crater of the volcano.
It will be dark in a few minutes. You aren't
strong enough, says Alfonso, you might be seized,
you might leap into the abyss.
Then he starts talking again about soya,
which will end starvation. Death is endless
and soothing. Why?

SONNET OF A FACE

In the heart a bullet, in the bullet an ape,
in the ape a plant, in the plant a mirror.
On envelopes and in the doors—a seal.
It holds together city streets by force.
Heaven's a hoop in which the plague begins.
A field of hounds, of emperors
on horseback, of drowning deer.
But not the one I seek, brother
with one heart, one antler. A castle
veduta, a goblin and gold, the swamp
of time and my attendants.
Arrow, you slipped away from me, I'll burn
until I hit you. Dead—
my life—I'll give it back to the city.

TO THE PRINCES OF DARKNESS

I doesn't dream, I stands up and leaves. Borges,
transposed by Pythagoras, sees gardens,
a garden each night, suburbs. The angels
of Kabbala let him sleep peacefully in
his house. When will I be an old man? Who keeps
entangling me in the flesh? Who opens
the door through which I (with
all the lavish and vulnerable
appendages: head, legs, watch, money)
crawls into the night? I've been robbed. What kind of
professionals drank up
all that was in my body, in my pockets,
on my skin? When I reach the edge, I lock up
my soul. I watch these sephirots,
hounds on the chase. They turn me over.
They let me turn them over. This
policeman, these mythic children
can kill with a smile. They're in a panic.
They feel, they know the hidden, without knowing
what and where it is. We're all in a panic.
The earth lives in a panic. You cannot even
dream by what I am, what I am.
I am safe because I do not know.
I am safe. I does not know. Who are you? Whom
do you serve? Are you still
immaculate? Speak,
Šalamun! When will I be a blessèd
old man, so that you'll stop
meddling with his
worn-out body?

TELL THE PEOPLE

Roosters sing.
A woman teaches a child the Greek alphabet.
A sparrow defecates.
In front of the window a flock of birds is flying.
MacGregor will go to Ljubljana as my messenger
at two o'clock. What am I doing
with this Australian kid?
April 13, 1978, on your birthday, I will
be in Zagreb, on Ilica, in the café
under the skyscraper at 10:30 A.M.
"Under my arm I will have sandals for
David, Ana, and you."
Zagreb is my native town.
If you're not there, I will go
to Šalata, in front of the house where I was born.
My wife fought for me very hard.
She almost killed two people,
Peter Trias and Ron Donovan.
Ron is here now. He came from Alaska,
where he was a fisherman and a carpenter
all those years. He had written a poem
in Knossos, the first after the one he wrote
in Pisa in 1970, when we first met.
I was living in the hotel Ariston
near the tower. When Maruška
came to Pisa she didn't find
either the tower or my house. It took her
two hours to drive around town, as in a
death dance. Ron was waiting eight years.
Wherever I go people fall for me.

Here in Paleohora we live as Gauguin
and Van Gogh lived in Arles.
I cannot translate anymore.

The flight of a bird is neither light nor terrible.
My name is neither bright nor dark.

On the terrace a girl will sing,
knowing nothing.

When I crawl around
this forest, naked, like
an animal,

I feel the world.

I will change into
the grasses.
When I am eaten up by

the worms,
they will turn everything,
as I do,

into gold.

FEAST

By the way of all spheres,
on steep rocks overgrown with segments of color,
covered with chalk that children have broken,
we watch fragments
that keep rising,
compressed as if under the weight of water,
their slow takeoff: a signpost,
white curtains raised.

There is no hardship in breathing,
precisely here, in this circle,
no hardship in breathing,
and also onward, ahead, it seems
as if balance is built in, unbreakable;
each time widening caves,
widening and narrowing,
like the activity of an unknown (unimaginable)
respiratory system, magnified under a microscope.

Invalid are nostalgia, night, melancholy,
laughter falling as snow,
everything parallel, everything there that can be
reached from here, all "the way" in between.

We are watching the reactions to this condition,
slowly, step by step, the outer leaves of the artichoke
float away.
We can imprint optional memories of notions.

There was a circle.
There was one just because we could not
use it.

Whatever the notion, they are all concentrically
disposed, far and near.
A freckle that was once an elevator
is *a priori* a ray, secured by intangibility.
Initiation is incredibly slow work,
similar to the turning of summer, winter, and stars.

Is this about how we have eaten?
Did we make a meal each time?

Enough so that in the process a tiny crack is left
and everything regenerates incredibly fast, and therefore now is.

You who keep a diary of growth and victims,
look!
Maybe many of them can read it,
light falls around,
only here of course nothing falls, it gets out.
The center, the source of energy watched by us
during this procedure, is empty. The cosmos makes the
    locus vanish,
eats it up. Energy, not consciousness, jumps across, (is)
in the negative. Therefore *everything* is in something,
what roughly, because of a notion, can be described
as a grain of sand, all space the remainder,
like dust after sawing wood.

On one cubic micron there are endless
galaxies, *each* with this enormous
space; nights, moons, suns, with constellations
that confound us, compressing our membrane.
The intergalactic and, of course, these
"injected" communications, too, are only oppression.

Along this window, in this window
there are innumerable other civilizations,
innumerable other cosmological systems.
Thus suffering does not matter,
layers do.

This is what I show here.

INDEX OF POEMS AND
TRANSLATORS

What's your favorite color... —*poet and Christopher Merrill*
When I crawl around... —*Michael Biggins*
Whoever eats from... —*poet and Christopher Merrill*
Words—*poet and Christopher Merrill*
You're a cry... —*poet and Phillis Levin*
Žare—*poet and Christopher Merrill*